FEB. 1 2 1997

DECADES

The
FIFTIES

Tom Stacy

STECK-VAUGHN
L I B R A R Y
Austin, Texas

DECADES

The Fifties
The Sixties
The Seventies
The Eighties

**Published in the United States in 1990
by Steck-Vaughn Co., Austin, Texas,**
a subsidary of the National
Education Corporation

First published in 1989 by
Wayland (Publishers) Ltd

© Copyright 1989 Wayland (Publishers) Ltd

Edited by Roger Coote
Designed by Helen White

Series Consultant: Stuart Laing
Dean of Cultural and Community Studies
University of Sussex

Consultant, American Edition: Jack Nelson
Graduate School of Education
Rutgers University

Library of Congress Cataloging-in-Publication Data
Stacy, Tom.
   The fifties.

   (Decades)
   Includes bibliographical references.
   Summary: Discusses the culture and historical events of the
1950s, covering the media, leisure, and such incidents as the
Korean War, civil rights, the Hungarian uprising, and the polio
vaccine.
   1. Social history—1945-1960—Juvenile literature. 2. United
States—Social conditions—1945—Juvenile literature. 3. United
States—Social life and customs—1945-1970—Juvenile literature.
[1. United States—History—1953-1961. 2. History, Modern—1945-
. 3. Popular culture—History—20th century]
I. Title. II. Series.
HN17.5.S73   1990   306'.0973'09045   89-21662
ISBN 0-8114-4212-8

Typeset by Multifacit, Keyport, N.J.
Printed in Italy
Bound by Lake Book Manufacturing
Melrose Park, Ill.

2 3 4 5 6 7 8 9 0 LB 94 93 92 91

Contents

INTRODUCTION

I n 1950 the world was recovering from the devastation of World War II (1939–45), which had ended five years earlier. The United States had emerged from the war as an undisputed "superpower" while much of Europe lay in ruins. Defeated Germany was divided in two and, until 1952, occupied by the Allies on one side and the Soviet Union on the other. The Russians had lowered an "iron curtain" across the continent, dividing East from West. In Asia, Japan (Germany's wartime ally) was rebuilding its shattered cities and factories. India had been an independent republic for just three years, while most of Africa was still ruled by colonial powers.

Above *Dining out fifties-style. A couple on a date listen to a swing band while they eat.*

The fifties were a time of great political tension and change. The peace that followed the war did not last long: the Korean War broke out in 1950. In 1952 the first hydrogen bomb was exploded at Eniwetok Atoll in the Pacific, followed a year later by one in the Soviet Union. The nuclear arsenals of East and West grew throughout the decade and the "Cold War" kept tensions high. In Britain, the Campaign for Nuclear Disarmament (CND) was founded in 1958 to press for the abolition of nuclear weapons. Independence movements came to the fore in Asia and Africa. In Europe the European Economic Community (EEC) was founded in 1957, to unite the continent for trade purposes.

In the 1950s the United States was already the wealthiest nation on earth and the American way of life was envied throughout the Western world. Meanwhile, to grow up in Europe was to move from the austerity, shortages, and rationing of the postwar period to a new era of material affluence.

To be young in 1950 was to be young in a world where "youth culture" hardly existed. Young people were expected to conform, and to behave according to the values dictated by their elders. Most of them did so, although a growing spirit of rebellion and a new assertiveness of ideas and styles soon developed.

During the fifties the standard of living rose steadily. Unemployment was low. People longed for a brighter, more lively world, and gradually things began to happen. Mainly the young led the way. Young people were an increasingly important market for clothes and other goods. They developed their own tastes in music and fashion. They began to express their own opinions more forcibly. The term "teenager" became familiar in English-speaking nations on both sides of the Atlantic.

Below *London in the early fifties was slowly recovering from the effects of wartime bombing. Large areas of the city still looked like this. The Barbican Center later rose from these ruins.*

Above *Americans enjoy a beach clambake. Wartime shortages didn't affect life in the United States as severely as in Europe. In the fifties the standard of living rose rapidly. The American way of life was envied and emulated.*

In the space of ten years, a far-reaching social revolution had developed. Its roots lay in the disruption of war, but its driving force came from the economic growth and technological advances of the West. The changes that took place in the 1950s were perhaps more noticeable than those of any succeeding decade. Their effects were felt everywhere—in the United States and Canada, in Britain, in Europe, in Australia and New Zealand, in Africa and Asia.

By 1960, the car dominated life in America, and was beginning to do the same in Europe. The space age had just begun with the launch of the world's first space satellite in 1957 by the Soviet Union. There were nuclear-powered submarines beneath the seas and nuclear power stations generating electricity on land. The British Empire had become a new, more loosely knit "family of nations" called the Commonwealth. Television had become the center of home entertainment and information, pushing aside the movies and newspapers. People were eager to buy the growing assortment of consumer and luxury goods—radios, televisions, washing machines, refrigerators, and gadgets of every kind. "All Shook Up" was a pop hit of the decade, and its title seems to symbolize what had happened to the world. The age of austerity had been replaced by the affluent society.

Above *A fifties advertisement for vacuum cleaners and washing machines. The manufacturers appealed directly to women in the home, promising to abolish household drudgery, especially the old-fashioned "wash day".*

FASHION

Above *High fashion for the well-to-do. French fashion designer Pierre Balmain shows off a reversible evening cloak, 1950.*

During the long war years of the forties, people had been deprived of fashion. When peacetime came and production gradually got back to normal, a generation of young men and women looked eagerly to fashion designers for new styles. Unless you were rich, there was disappointingly little to be excited about at first. "High fashion" remained dominated by the expensive fashion houses—such as Christian Dior, Chanel, and Pierre Balmain in Paris. Their original *haute couture* designs were far too expensive for most shoppers, but they were copied in cheaper materials by other fashion houses and sold in the department stores.

Children in the 1950s dressed differently from the way they do today. Jeans were seldom seen outside the western United States. Haircuts were short, often military-style ''crewcuts.'' In England boys wore short pants, at least until they were 12 or so. For a boy, his first pair of long pants was a symbol of manhood. Young girls seldom wore slacks to school. Their mothers dressed them in cotton dresses, or skirts, blouses, and cardigan sweaters. Bobby socks, saddle shoes, penny loafers, and full ''poodle'' skirts were standard items.

Teenagers tried to develop their own styles within the limited range of clothing available. There was an urge to show off and experiment. But few designers made clothing for the youth market. As the decade progressed stores in America opened departments that catered to the young. British youngsters had designers such as Mary Quant, for a fashion look that was bright, different, and affordable.

Fashion for girls

A tomboy might run around in long pants or jeans with the bottoms rolled up, but the average American teenage girl was more likely to go out on a date wearing a circular, full skirt over a stiffened crinoline petticoat, short "bobby socks," and flat shoes. High, stiletto heels came a little later. Eventually, fashion designers and manufacturers realized a startling fact: two-thirds of the female population of the United States was under 30. There was a huge market waiting to be tapped.

Movies and television had a big influence on what young girls wore. Some young women wore tight sweaters in imitation of movie stars like Jane Russell and Jayne Mansfield. Another

Above *Fifties cover girl supreme: Marilyn Monroe. This cover photo from a July 1956 Illustrated magazine accentuates her "sex-symbol" role and also illustrates the ideal look to which readers might aspire.*

Above *A fifties couple jiving. Dancing swirls out the bell-like skirt of the young woman's typical check print dress. The casual look of her partner characterizes the leisure menswear of the period.*

star, Marilyn Monroe, became the international pin up of the decade, her face and figure widely displayed. Sales of padded bras soared. The French coined the descriptive term: *le busty-look américain.*

The typical fifties look was tight-waisted, the swinging skirt worn with a belt and a shirt-style blouse. Wide skirts were fine for jiving—the favorite teenage dance of the time. Girls' hairstyles were generally softly curled. The poodle cut and pony tail were popular hair styles; another was the head band. Toward the end of the fifties the puffed-up, back-combed (teased) "beehive" styles became fashionable and was adopted by young and old alike.

New materials

The real revolution in fashion lay not so much in the look, as in the materials. Science had entered the textile mills. Synthetic materials such as Orlon, Acrilan, Dacron, and Poplin—developed following the breakthrough invention of nylon in the 1930s—were taking over from traditional wool and cotton. They were cheaper and they could be dyed in many colors. Many were "drip dry," making wash day less of a chore. The new materials were especially popular for underwear and men's shirts. Women wore nylon stockings which were becoming cheaper than silk ones and less liable to snag and develop runs. Pantyhose did not become popular until the sixties.

Above *Young sharp dressers in the London of 1955. Elements of the teddy boy style are worn by the cigarette-smoking boy: velvet collar and suede shoes; missing are the "Edwardian" drainpipe trousers and string tie.*

Teenage boys

There had been little change in men's appearance throughout the forties. In the fifties, a new freedom was apparent, even though for many males standard acceptable dress was still a suit and tie or sports jacket and gray flannel trousers. Young men slicked down their hair with hair cream. The traditional "short back and sides" haircut was still the norm, but it gradually gave way to longer styles with high waves in the front and short crewcuts. Fewer young men wore hats, though older men still wore them. If you watch a thirties or forties newsreel, you will see very few men without a cap or hat.

In America, Marlon Brando's film *The Wild One* helped popularize a more "anti-social" fashion—the leather look of the biker or "greaser." The overall effect aimed at a combination of toughness and "streetwise" smartness. There were silly, and short-lived, fashion crazes: the Walt Disney movie *Davy Crockett* inspired a brief fashion for wearing coonskin hats. Recording stars were also influential as fashion-makers. Most of all, boys imitated Elvis Presley, whose image ranged from a "macho man" in tight-jeans to a dandy in gold lamé suits encrusted with sparkling sequins and glittering jewelry.

In Britain, some youths took to wearing "Edwardian" style clothes; hence the nickname "teddy boy." They wore knee-length jackets, narrow "drainpipe" trousers, bootlace ties, gaudy fluorescent socks, and thick crepe-soled shoes known as "creepers." Teddy boys were very particular about their hair which was worn long, greased, and swept back, usually with a wave at the front.

During the fifties, men's fashions moved steadily into the limelight. Another important feature of the decade was that young people in general were becoming self-aware, and a

ACRILAN

A FOR
AN
ACTIVE
LIFE!

Above *Fifties clothes were marketed as being stylish, long-wearing, and easy to care for. New fabrics with synthetic fibers rapidly replaced traditional fabrics.*

''generation gap'' was growing. No longer did the young rely on the taste of their elders. They had money in their pockets and a growing range of goods to choose from. They were self-confident, and determined to create their own styles. By so doing, they forced designers and manufacturers to follow popular taste rather than try to lead and create it as they had in the past.

POP MUSIC

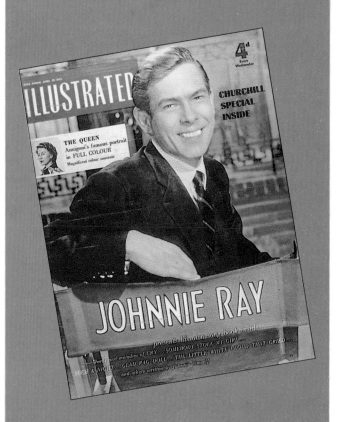

At the start of the fifties, rock music was still in its infancy. Country music, jazz, and blues, which were to influence the development of pop, were alive and well, but they were "minority" tastes. Mass-market music was dominated, as it had been throughout the 1930s and 1940s, by the songs from "Tin Pan Alley" (the Broadway musicals), the crooners, and the big bands.

The long-playing record had been invented in the United States in 1948. In 1950 LPs first went on sale in Britain. The days of the 78 rpm record were numbered. The 45 rpm single appeared soon after. In 1951 Johnnie Ray had a double-sided million seller with *Cry/Little White Cloud That Cried.* That same year Vera Lynn became the first British artist to top the U.S. charts, with a song called *Auf Wiedersehn Sweetheart.*

Above *This cover photo of singer Johnnie Ray, "Prince of Wails," illustrates his ability to arouse near-hysteria in fans.*

The charts on both sides of the Atlantic were packed with solo singers, male and female. Big names were Jo Stafford, Kay Starr, Doris Day, Guy Mitchell, Frankie Laine, Perry Como—and the megastars of their day—Bing Crosby and Frank Sinatra. For future millionaire stars born in 1950 (who included Peter Gabriel and Stevie Wonder) and 1951 (Sting and Phil Collins), there was not much to rock to in their cradles. However, as these fifties toddlers began to explore the world and their first day of school came nearer, the music scene was beginning to change.

The dawn of rock'n'roll

In 1955 Chuck Berry gained an introduction, via blues singer Muddy Waters, to Chess Records in Chicago. His first single was called *Maybelline*, and its arrival on the pop charts heralded the advent of the singer-guitarist. This type of artist had been confined mainly to country music and black music. In that same year, a record by a 28-year-old former hillbilly musician named Bill Haley reached number one on the charts all over the world. The event began a musical revolution that seemed, to some critics, likely to threaten the foundations of Western civilization!

The song was *Rock Around the Clock*, which had been featured in the movie *Blackboard Jungle*. On its second appearance, it took off and sold by the millions. Pop music was never to be the same again. Haley and his band, the Comets, were unlikely ''revolutionaries''—not exactly in the first bloom of youth. Nonetheless, showings of Haley films caused consternation among the readers of ''respectable'' newspapers as they learned of excited teenagers ''jiving'' in the aisles—during the screening! Some theaters banned the Haley films and some jukebox operators refused to stock rock records in their machines. In Connecticut a theater lost its license after a reported riot at a rock show hosted by disc jockey Alan Freed.

Bill Haley, the apparent cause of all this mayhem, must have been as surprised as anyone. His success was short-lived though, and his career declined after three or four years. Into the spotlight which he had momentarily occupied were to step some of the most exciting performers in pop history.

Below *Detroit-born Bill Haley moved from hillbilly music to rock'n'roll. Phrases such as ''See You Later Alligator,'' a 1956 Haley hit, entered the teenage vocabulary. The famous Haley kiss-curl was much copied.*

Above *Elvis Presley, rock'n'roll's greatest star, was the most photographed celebrity of the fifties. This shot was taken while filming* Love Me Tender, *1956.*

Legends of rock

In 1954 a Mississippi-born singer named Elvis Presley had recorded his first single, *That's All Right, Mama*. The world remained unmoved, but Presley's switch to the RCA record company in 1956 was the start of the most successful musical career in history. Presley's recording of *Heartbreak Hotel* hit the U.S. charts in April 1956. His appearance on television's *The Milton Berle Show* attracted a vast nationwide audience and he was immediately signed to a film contract.

The rock'n'roll wagon was rolling. Along came a host of performers whose names are now a part of pop history; Jerry Lee Lewis, Buddy Holly, the Everly Brothers, Gene Vincent, and Little Richard. The fans went wild over these "new wave" fifties pop stars. Even Johnnie Ray, who was really a middle of the road singer, attracted fervent mobs of fans during his 1956 Australian tour.

On the whole, planners of television programs in most countries were slow to react to the popularity of these new stars, and uncertain about how to present them when they did give them air time. Many teenagers tuned in to radio stations in order to hear their favorite music, and the chattering of the DJs (disc jockey).

As the second Bill Haley movie *Don't Knock the Rock* was released in 1957, new acts such as the Platters and Frankie Lymon and the Teenagers were drawing wild audiences of excited fans. Ricky Nelson made the transition from TV star to teenage idol, and Buddy Holly and the Crickets at last got their big hit with *That'll Be the Day*.

Above *Texan Buddy Holly's career began in 1954, singing on local radio. His hallmarks were horn-rimmed glasses and a Fender Stratocaster guitar. In 1958 Holly split with his backing group, the Crickets. He died in 1959.*

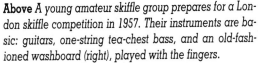

Above *A young amateur skiffle group prepares for a London skiffle competition in 1957. Their instruments are basic: guitars, one-string tea-chest bass, and an old-fashioned washboard (right), played with the fingers.*

A British phenomenon was skiffle; a "do-it-yourself" music loosely derived from American country and folk. Youngsters got together to form skiffle groups with such unlikely instruments as washboards and basses made from wooden tea chests. The leading skiffle star was ex-jazzman Lonnie Donegan whose hits included *Cumberland Gap* and *Puttin' on the Style*. The year was 1957, and in Liverpool John Lennon and Paul McCartney met for the first time, possibly listening to the number one American hit, Pat Boone's syrupy ballad, *Love Letters in the Sand*. They, and thousands of other young people, were picking up guitars and dreaming of stardom. A dream that was to come true for Lennon and McCartney.

In 1958 Elvis Presley was drafted into the U.S. Army. Fans mourned, but for the Army it was a public relations opportunity not to be missed. Cameras followed the new recruit everywhere as Elvis had his hair cut and abandoned his gold lamé jacket for an army uniform. His time in the service did not hinder his career one bit; his 1958 hit, *Jailhouse Rock*, was a worldwide hit, and it entered the British charts at number one as soon as it appeared, the first record ever to do so.

Apart from all this rock excitement, the 1950s saw some other notable musical landmarks. Harry Belafonte's *Mary's Boy Child* was a massive Christmas hit in 1957. Belafonte, a New Yorker, became one of the most respected black entertainers, as a singer-songwriter and actor. A 1958 hit was *On the Street Where You Live* by Vic Damone, a song from the Lerner and Loewe smash-hit Broadway musical, *My Fair Lady*. Harold Jenkins chose one of the least likely stage names—Conway Twitty—and still ran up a string of hits, from the 1950s to the early 1980s. 1958 saw the solitary single hit, *Donna*, by Richie Valens, a 17-year-old Hispanic American who was to be killed in the 1959 air crash which also took the lives of DJ-turned-singer The Big Bopper and the great Buddy Holly. Holly's *It Doesn't Matter Anymore* was an immediate posthumous hit.

Toward the sixties

The 1950s seemed to end on a downbeat note. Alan Freed was fired from his radio and TV jobs for refusing to declare that he had never taken ''payola,'' bribes from record companies. Jazz singer Billie Holiday died in July 1959 as a result of drug and alcohol abuse.

However, there were hopeful signs for the future. After almost two years Elvis Presley was about to leave the Army and return to the recording studio. In 1959 Berry Gordy, Jr. founded Motown records, a company that was to play a significant role over the next ten years of pop

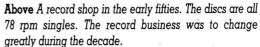

Above *A record shop in the early fifties. The discs are all 78 rpm singles. The record business was to change greatly during the decade.*

music. Record players had only recently become popular and affordable. Vinyl discs were, at the time, the only medium on which to buy recorded music; cassettes and CDs were yet to be invented. Most recordings were mono, although stereo records first went on sale in 1958, resulting in an enormous sale of new sound equipment for years to come. There was to be a massive explosion of pop music in the decade to come.

THE MEDIA

Model CT1381 In Primrose Yellow; also available in Sea Mist Green or White.

During the fifties, almost all areas of the media changed dramatically. Newspapers and magazines became glossier, with pictures growing both larger and more numerous. Headlines became bolder and more sensational. The paperback book, with its modest price, increasingly replaced traditional hardcover editions. The number of radio listeners fell, and so did audiences in movie theaters. Only television went from weakness to strength.

Above *Advertising had growing power to influence consumer choice. Customers were eager to buy newly available goods, like this refrigerator.*

Magazines and newspapers

Few magazines were aimed directly at young people, apart from comics and a few more serious children's magazines such as *Jack and Jill* and *Highlights for Children*. When readers got too old for *Superman* comics they simply moved on to the daily paper. Advertisers were mainly interested in reaching the family at home, rather than the young. Incomes were rising, and though few married women went out to work, women generally were an increasingly attractive target for media advertising. Magazines were full of advertisements enticing people to buy clothes, furniture, cosmetics, children's needs, and the expanding range of domestic appliances.

Teenagers might turn to the readers' letters in newspapers and magazines, where "personal problems" ranging from acne to sex were discreetly discussed. There were no "frank discussion" radio phone-in shows in the 1950s; the advice columns of newspapers and magazines were still almost the only place where people could air subjects that were not talked about in the family or in school classrooms. Some subjects—homosexuality, or birth control for instance—were not even mentioned in these advice columns.

The fifties were a golden age of sports heroes—the Harlem Globetrotters basketball team, Mickey Mantle in baseball, tennis players "Little Mo" Connolly and Lew Hoad, Rocky Marciano the boxer, jockey Gordon Richards, and four-minute miler Roger Bannister among them. On the whole the press treated the stars with great respect, and there were few shocking stories exposing the seamier side of professional sports.

Left *By running the first sub-four-minute mile at Oxford in 1954, medical student Roger Bannister became one of sport's most famous names. Newspapers all over the world carried photos of the record-breaking run.*

Sports attracted much media interest, and so did crime. Murders made the news, especially when most convicted murderers faced the death penalty. Show-biz gossip was popular, too. Movie stars, rather than pop singers, hit the headlines.

Radio had stolen from the newspapers their claim to be "first with the news" and television was challenging radio for that position. Newspapers responded by increasing the amount of commentary. Regular columnists were as well known as the hosts of today's television talk shows.

Radio

In the United States the airwaves were hotly contested by numerous small local commercial stations, operating alongside the major national networks such as CBS and NBC. Small stations were quick to respond to changes in public taste, and eager to satisfy advertising sponsors that they were moving with the times. It was North America that created the DJ, transforming radio from a words-with-music broadcasting medium to a mainly-music format on many stations. As older people switched from radio to TV, programmers quickly switched to music-hungry youth as the new radio audience.

In Britain radio remained a monopoly of the BBC (British Broadcasting Corporation). There was no commercial radio (nor commercial television) until 1955. Records were seldom heard on BBC radio, other than on request programs such as *Housewives' Choice and Children's Favourites*. The programs consisted mostly of talks and plays, light music ranging from Latin American bands to organ solos, and variety and comedy half-hours. One wavelength was devoted to broadcasting "serious" music and drama.

The fifties witnessed the end for traditional

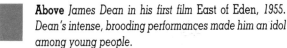
Above *James Dean in his first film* East of Eden, *1955. Dean's intense, brooding performances made him an idol among young people.*

mass-audience radio entertainment. Popular radio comedians, such as Jack Benny, had been on radio since the 1930s. However, a new trend was emerging. Radio audiences were falling steadily as more and more people bought television sets. Before long, Jack Benny had also moved to the TV screen.

The silver screen

Motion pictures were most popular just after World War II. Hollywood glitter, Hollywood stars, and Hollywood movies made news all over the world. But during the fifties movie audiences became smaller and smaller as the new medium of television took over.

As the movie theaters lost their older audiences, who preferred to stay at home and watch TV quiz shows, Westerns, or crime series, they became more reliant on the "teen-and-twenty" market. This led to the production of more films that catered to a specific "youth appeal."

Moviemakers had already begun to examine the problems of young people caught between innocence and experience. During the fifties some adults feared that the movie industry was helping to bring about the breakdown of civilized life. Films with titles such as *Motorcycle Gang* tried to cash in on these concerns, and also draw in a young audience. The young responded enthusiastically to the new acting talents of Marlon Brando and James Dean. Dean in particular, through his two films *East of Eden* and *Rebel Without a Cause*, became a symbol of youthful rebellion. He died tragically at the age of 24 in a car crash, but his reputation and popularity is still very much alive with young people today.

The "family film" became less commercially viable, despite the continued success of the Walt Disney studios with "real-life" nature films, children's classics, and animated cartoons. Movie studios turned instead to shock and horror, with a growing output of "adult

Below *Though older than James Dean, Marlon Brando had an equally great appeal to young movie audiences. Films such as* The Wild One *and* On the Waterfront *established his screen persona as rebellious.*

Above *A scene from the 1955 science-fiction thriller* This Island Earth. *The theme of humanity threatened by hostile aliens was a fifties favorite with moviemakers. The best of such films are now cult classics.*

only'' films. Science fiction movies were popular, perhaps because people were worried about the ''progress'' of science. They were especially concerned about the atomic bomb, and the threat of Communism, symbolically represented in films by terrifying aliens attempting to take over the world. Mad scientists featured in a number of films, usually turning themselves into monsters as a result of their misguided experiments and research. Some of the fifties science fiction classics, such as *The Incredible Shrinking Man* (1957), *This Island Earth* (1955), *Invasion of the Bodysnatchers* (1956), and *Invaders from Mars* (1953), are still winning fresh audiences when shown today.

By the mid-fifties the Hollywood bubble had burst. Most of the major studios were turning to television, and many movie theaters were facing closure as audiences dwindled. By 1957 audience figures were slumping disastrously. There was a real fear that the younger generation would drift away from movies entirely—despite the attraction of the movie theater and drive-in movie for teenagers seeking privacy on a date.

The movies turned to technology in an attempt to compete with TV. Various ''wide screen'' systems, such as Cinerama and Vistavision, were introduced to entice audiences. Another, less successful, innovation was the 3-D movie, for which audiences were issued special glasses. Despite the undoubted thrill of being able to get a realistic view of the Creature from the Black Lagoon, 3-D films did not win

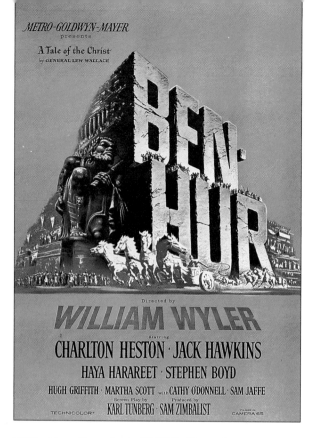

back the vanishing movie audience. Not even such blockbuster epics as *Ben Hur* (1959) could lure the viewers away from their homes and their TV sets.

The small screen

TV created new stars, such as Phil Silvers, who played Sergeant Bilko, and boosted the careers of film actresses such as Lucille Ball, of the long-running *I Love Lucy* series. At the beginning of the fifties, television was still finding its feet, still copying radio and films, unaware of its own huge potential. Television, like radio, did not see the young as an important target audience. The first impact of rock'n'roll came from records played on small radio stations and the film *Rock Around the Clock*. Only after the craze had taken off did television producers lift their restrictions and allow the rock stars in front of the camera.

The fifties was the decade in which, for many people, television began to be more "real" than real life. It had a power that movies lacked—it brought the everyday world into people's homes.

In 1951 American war hero General Douglas MacArthur made a triumphant tour of the United States. Cities like Chicago staged "MacArthur Days" to greet him and large crowds jammed the streets. Few spectators in the street could actually see MacArthur, and they grumbled that those who had stayed at home to watch on TV were getting a much better view of what was happening. TV viewers got close-ups from strategically positioned cameras and were constantly told by the broadcast-

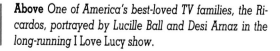

Above *The coronation of Queen Elizabeth II in Westminster Abbey, June 2, 1953. For the first time, TV cameras broadcast the historic ceremony.*

ers that this was a "great event." Pictures of waving, cheering crowds were shown. In fact, most of these shots showed people waving to the camera—being on television had become more important than merely seeing a famous person drive by in a car.

Television broadcasters were beginning to see how they could present, and even control, certain events. The coronation of Queen Elizabeth II in 1953, for instance, was televised live, but only after much argument. Traditionalists fiercely opposed the "intrusion" of the cameras, with their cables and other paraphernalia, into London's Westminster Abbey. Those in favor of televising the ceremony argued, convincingly, that television would add to the occasion by making people throughout Britain and the Commonwealth feel part of the great day.

When it was televised, viewers throughout the world were treated to a first-hand coverage of the royal ceremony. No one since has ever seriously argued against televising such an important event.

In the fifties the organization and timing of sporting events were still left to the sports bodies, with TV and radio admitted as privileged onlookers and reporters. The televising of major sports such as football, baseball, basketball, tennis, golf and other sports did much to increase their popularity. Few people believed that spectators would stay at home and watch their favorite sports on TV. Television could not yet match the thrill of actually being there; the screen was small, the picture black and white (and often shaky), and the camera techniques were very primitive.

Advertisers were quick to realize the potential of television. TV commercials with their catchy jingles, cartoons, and actors recommending the latest products became as popular as many of the programs. Politicians were more suspicious, however. During elections, they preferred "whistle-stop" nationwide tours and public meetings. When they did agree to appear on television, it was only for carefully controlled and formal "addresses." Interviewers were seldom permitted to tackle politicians head-on, and politicians rarely entered into televised debates with their rivals.

All this was to change with the 1960 Presidential election, which saw the famous TV debates between John Kennedy and Richard Nixon. Viewers were allegedly won over by Kennedy's relaxed style and youthful good looks which contrasted with the unfortunate Nixon's stubble-darkened complexion and tense manner. After the 1950s no politician could afford to ignore television. Politicians even started to develop advertisements to broadcast during "prime time."

LEISURE

In the fifties the leisure industry was just beginning its remarkable postwar growth. People had more free time as working weeks grew shorter and annual vacations longer. People also had more money to spend on activities they enjoyed. But at first the effects of this social change were slow to appear.

Above *The local dance hall on a Saturday night was the favorite meeting place for many fifties couples.*

Dancing

Music and dancing were as popular in the fifties as they are today. The usual spots were large dance halls, and the music was performed "live" by a dance band, with perhaps a smaller jazz or swing band to fill in. Couples danced together most of the time. The traditional ballroom favorites such as the waltz and fox-trot were played. Not everyone knew how to dance them correctly, and dance studios did good business giving lessons to teenagers seeking this essential social skill. The jive, a development of the 1940s jitterbug craze, was the dance that the young adopted as their own, dancing it to whatever music came along as long as it had the right tempo.

Sports and hobbies

Millions of spectators watched live sporting events. In the United States baseball and football were undergoing changes. Black players regularly featured on major league teams. Big money franchises were frequently gaining control of famous-name city teams. Two major New

Above *The scooter, cheaper than a motorcycle, provided low-cost mobility for young people who could not afford the luxury of a car. As in other fields of design, Italian models (Lambretta, Vespa) were very popular.*

York baseball teams—the Brooklyn Dodgers and the New York Giants—moved to Los Angeles and San Francisco. In Britain, soccer drew the largest crowds in its history. TV coverage of the Olympic Games (at Helsinki in 1952 and Melbourne in 1956) did much to increase worldwide interest in sports—even though live satellite transmissions were not yet available.

This new popularity of professional sports led to some players demanding, and receiving, much larger financial rewards. Sports prowess in high school offered the prospect of a college scholarship and maybe a lucrative professional career.

While team sports thrived, there was also a growing interest in other pursuits, such as fishing, winter sports, hot rod racing, and surfing.

Above *New York Yankees baseball star Joe DiMaggio remained a popular hero throughout the fifties. Briefly married to Marilyn Monroe, he was elected to the Baseball Hall of Fame in 1955.*

But there were hardly any leisure centers or health clubs within the average teenager's price range. The beach and surf lifestyle of California was a million miles away from the streets of the big city. The local tennis or golf club, with its high membership fees, could look almost equally out of reach.

Many teenagers rode bicycles, and some went on to ride motorcycles. A major reason for working as a teenager was to save money to buy a car. At home, hobbies were often sexually stereotyped. Boys made models (airplanes were popular). Girls made clothes, sewed, and knitted. Collecting things—including stamps, coins, and baseball cards—was a passion (often short-lived); so too was writing letters to overseas pen-pals. Teenagers shared their parents' enthusiasm for watching television; it was new.

Below *As this 1953 New York Central Railroad advertisement shows, the railroads still aimed to attract the long-distance traveler. Competition with airlines intensified with the jet age, and the railroads declined.*

Long and Short of Smart Travel

... New York Central style!

Make long jumps on a roomy, restful dieseliner . . . with New York Central to do the driving. Step off fresh, and find a drive-ur-self car ready for short runs at your destination.
Ask your ticket agent to reserve a car for you. Then on your way, instead of grueling hours at the wheel, you can relax in New York Central comfort.

The comfort of conditioned air in a Pullman hotel-room-on-wheels or a streamlined coach with deep, lean-back seats. The comfort of refreshments in the lounge and delicious meals at a dining car table.
Best of all, enjoy the comfort of the Water Level Route . . . through gentle, scenic valleys between East and West.

Make distance just a dream . . . rather than the strain of facing headlights hour after hour. Sleep your way on New York Central . . . yet have a car for your personal use when you arrive.

Travel and vacations

A major difference between the fifties and today is that far fewer people traveled. An overseas vacation was still the preserve of the very rich. Places such as the French Riviera or Venice were just picture postcard names to most people. A survey taken in 1954 found that about 15 percent of all adult Americans had never traveled more than 250 miles from their homes. The majority of Americans had never even seen the Atlantic or Pacific Oceans. Many American families went by car on "motor trips" to lakes, mountains, or resorts for their vacations.

The majority of Americans took their vacations within North America. Mexico or Canada represented the farthest many ever traveled.

In other countries travel was still somewhat limited to within national borders. Australians went to the beach. Britons too went to the seashore, usually by rail or bus. Holiday camps were a popular destination for many; two weeks of "organized" rest and recreation at a coastal resort, with fun and games provided throughout the day and night, a babysitter for the children in the evening, and everything included in one price. Cheap jet travel had not yet made possible the package vacation by air. Apart from those people who traveled abroad as part of their military service relatively few people had ever set foot on foreign soil.

When people ate in a restaurant, they were unlikely to try foreign food. There were comparatively few "ethnic" restaurants outside the largest cities, and the fast food chains were unheard of outside the United States. For fifties diners, there was one innovation: Muzak or "canned music." The Muzak company had begun to develop in the 1930s and by the 1950s had expanded its services so much that background "music" could be heard not only in restaurants and hotels, but in beauty salons, supermarkets, factories, and even cemeteries.

Above *A 1950 Coca-Cola advertisement featuring a giant automated vending machine. The familiar red soda machine spread from the U.S. all over the world as American eating and drinking habits became international.*

YOUTH CULTURE

Teenagers only began to emerge as a distinct group in society during the 1940s. In the 1950s adults first began to express concern, even alarm, at the growth of "gang culture." This undesirable phenomenon was blamed on the development of rock'n'roll, and on the relaxation in discipline both at homes and in the schools that had been brought about by World War II and its aftermath.

Above *The fifties dream: the gleaming chrome-plated car represented glamour and the good life to which many teenagers aspired.*

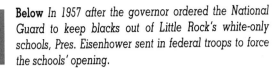

Below *In 1957 after the governor ordered the National Guard to keep blacks out of Little Rock's white-only schools, Pres. Eisenhower sent in federal troops to force the schools' opening.*

Racial violence was all too familiar in the United States, where the fifties witnessed an upsurge in blacks' demands for civil rights. World War II had caused considerable unrest among black Americans—especially those suffering unfair working practices at home and those serving in the army. The fifties saw renewed demands for action, and young blacks were prominent in the campaign—for example, in seeking to register as students in colleges that had previously refused to admit blacks. The Reverend Martin Luther King, Jr. became leader of the civil rights movement in 1956. A successful boycott of whites-only buses in Montgomery, Alabama, overturned the city's segregation policy. On May 17, 1954, the U.S. Supreme Court ruled that any separation of school pupils because of their race was unconstitutional. But it was to be another decade before southern states completely abandoned segregation in the public schools. Progress toward desegregation was swifter in colleges and universities, and more college-educated blacks entered the world of work demanding the jobs

and opportunities for which they were now qualified through education and training.

Racism was hardly limited to the United States. In Britain there was a shortage of labor in certain areas—public transport and nursing, for example—and immigration from the Caribbean was encouraged to meet the shortage. Few nonwhite immigrants had settled in Britain before the fifties. In London and some other cities where the West Indian newcomers settled, they came up against a "color bar," particularly when they tried to rent housing. White Teddy boys promoted an outbreak of racial violence in London's Notting Hill district. The "riot," a minor incident in itself, was a shock to many, and a warning to all.

Hanging around, having fun

Getting a job was not too difficult for the teenagers of the fifties. But, although this meant that they had money to spend, there was little entertainment specifically for them. Youth clubs and

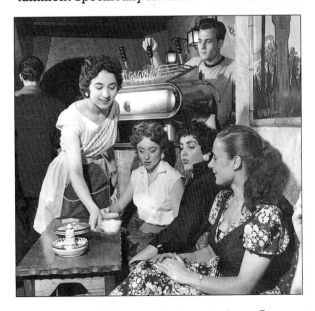

Above *A "Spanish-style" fifties coffee house. For many young people, the noise of the hissing espresso coffee machine became a familiar accompaniment to jukebox music and conversation.*

organizations were popular; most American teenagers belonged to some kind of club. Soda fountains and luncheonettes with juke boxes provided popular meeting places. Although many college-age young men proved their manhood by consuming large quantities of beer, to be drunk on the street still carried a social stigma. In many families, it was frowned on for a woman to smoke outside the home. Such behavior was "not nice." The health hazards of cigarette smoking were not widely recognized, and most teenagers quickly followed their elders into the smoking habit. They were encouraged by numerous cigarette ads on television extolling the sophisticated lifestyle portrayed by smoking. Very few young people took, or even knew about drugs.

Permissiveness

Despite growing affluence, young people had considerably less freedom in the fifties than they have today. Most lived at home until they got married, went into the armed forces, or perhaps went to college. Parents issued "house rules" and expected that these would be obeyed. How you styled your hair, what you wore, where you went, and how late you came home at night: any of these could start an argument. If the rules were broken, punishment usually involved "being grounded" which meant being forbidden to go out for a number of days. You were not really considered an adult until you were 21 and allowed to vote.

The fifties marked the very beginnings of the so-called "permissive age." A girl might expect to be kissed on a first date or else she would wonder if there was something wrong with her. She might allow a boy to "go further" if she liked him enough, and after three or four months dating together she would assume they were "going steady" and begin to think of getting engaged. Marriage was the goal: to be un-

married was thought "odd," though two unmarried men could share a home without their neighbors assuming, rightly or wrongly, that they were lovers. To be an unmarried mother was almost as scandalous as to be homosexual, yet an increasing number of unmarried young girls were becoming pregnant. The birth control pill had not yet been developed and ig-

Above The beatniks of the fifties "dropped out" of conventional society to pursue free-thinking artistic and intellectual life styles. The beatnik movement influenced young people to adopt a more radical, questioning approach to life.

norance in sexual matters was commonplace. Sex education was rarely taught in the schools.

The sexual revolution was only just beginning, and few people would have known what "sexual stereotyping" referred to. Although women were active in many fields, and were working to increase opportunities for women, few girls questioned their role as future wives and mothers. Most were still looking for jobs, not careers, and a relatively small proportion of female high school students went on to college. But the numbers were growing, and the women's movement was on its way.

Finding a voice

To many adults "youth culture" meant "gangs." Greasers, with their distinctive dress, seemed a visible symbol of a new and antisocial phenomenon. Hell's Angels racing along the superhighways on huge motorcycles also made good headlines in newspapers, often attracting more outrage than their activities warranted. Teenage crime was on the increase, and the teenage gangs of the 1957 hit musical *West Side Story* had their real-life counterparts. Vandalism in cities was a growing concern, but organized violence (soccer hooliganism, for example) was practically unknown. Most young people were conventional and unquestioning. Organizations such as the Girl and Boy Scouts enjoyed a popularity they have not had since.

Teenagers got together to have fun and share interests. Boys went to clubs to meet girls, and vice versa. Australians and Americans living in the sun belt went to the beach and had barbecues. Blacks and whites tended to socialize separately.

Those belonging to what the media called "ban the bomb" or "beatnik" groups met in dimly lit coffee houses—their casual dress, long hair, and beards proclaiming their "pro-

Below *"If we can't afford a shiny new car, let's decorate an old one just the way we want." Teenagers were often portrayed as cheerful, active, and involved in such harmless pursuits as this.*

test." "Beat" philosophy—pacifism, mysticism, anarchy, free love, socialism, and so on—was to have a great influence during the sixties. Its most famous figure was the writer and drop-out Jack Kerouac, author of *On the Road* (1957). The fifties beats, a subterranean generation of writers, artists, and eccentrics, were the forerunners of the protesters and hippies of the next generation.

Youth was still struggling to find a voice in the fifties. It was not taken seriously by the media, but the seeds of the sixties revolution were being sown. Class barriers were beginning to erode, as young people from different backgrounds mixed more, particularly in the expanding universities and colleges. The post-war "baby boom" was creating a new generation with fresh hopes.

STYLE

To a teenager of today transported back in time, a fifties town would look familiar yet strangely different. The cars were bigger then, more angular, with tailfins, lots of chrome, and bulbous headlights. Cars did not even have seat belts yet. Steam railroad locomotives hissed and puffed into the local station. Stores in most parts of the world had over-the-counter service; the supermarket was an American innovation of the 1930s and was only just beginning to appear elsewhere.

Above *Many stores were still small, like this 1954 example. The owner served customers from behind the counter.*

Below *Americans enjoyed growing economic prosperity after World War II. Supermarket shelves were stacked with food of a price and quality unrivaled elsewhere.*

gleaming skyscraper making bold use of dark glass. This vision, of a tall glass tower, was to be endlessly imitated by lesser architects as American cities grew higher, more office buildings were added to downtown areas. At the same time cities in other countries began to expand by demolishing old sections or rebuildings areas destroyed during World War II.

The "high-rise" building explosion was just beginning to make its mark on architecture outside the United States. One of the most powerful influences on building style in the fifties was Brutalism, a school of architecture that made few concessions to classical ideas of style or beauty. Huge concrete piers held up slablike apartment buildings—topped by an undisguised water tank.

London's skyline was still dominated by the dome of St. Paul's Cathedral, as it had been for almost 300 years, but the gaps made by wartime bombing were soon to be filled with an undistinguished jumble of concrete and glass. Australia's modern capital, Canberra, was more fortunate. Its development was controlled by a commission set up by the Australian government in 1958.

Skylines

The fifties produced some of the best work of architects such as Buckminster Fuller, the American who became known as the "Space-Age designer" for his mathematical domes which looked as if they could as easily stand on the surface of Mars as in Missouri. It was also the age of Frank Lloyd Wright's Guggenheim Museum in New York (1959) with its coil-like sweeps and ramps, as well as of Le Corbusier's chapel of Notre-Dame du Haut at Ronchamp, France (1956).

Mies van der Rohe's Seagram Building in New York (1958) is a famous fifties building, a

Above *Swiss-born architect Le Corbusier (Charles Edouard Jeanneret, 1887-1965) designed the chapel of Notre-Dame du Haut at Ronchamp in France. It was praised for its daring use of simple lines and shapes.*

Design for the home

The fifties saw a new interest in good design, in engineering, and in manufacturing generally. The Festival of Britain (1951) and the Brussels World Fair (1958) helped to encourage new ideas. Britain's Festival was a huge success, as people flocked to the different pavilions on the South Bank in London. There were new designs to admire; steel-rod chairs, colorful fabrics, plastic tableware, convertible sofa-beds, and domestic appliances. Designers and interior decorators were starting to combine art with new developments in technology and the results were exciting.

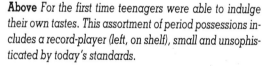

Above *For the first time teenagers were able to indulge their own tastes. This assortment of period possessions includes a record-player (left, on shelf), small and unsophisticated by today's standards.*

Swedish styling was admired for its simplicity and "functionalism"—things worked because they were designed to do so. The Scandinavian style used light softwoods in place of the traditional dark hardwoods for furniture and brought a softer, more rounded look to interiors. Magazine advertising played a key role in bringing new designs to people's attention, encouraging them to buy. The kitchen was a main target area—especially in Britain, where so many people were being rehoused after the war. Many had never had the opportunity of owning a "fitted kitchen." A greater interest in good design made it possible for even a small kitchen to be replanned on modern lines, with cupboard space, refrigerator, washing machine, and other modern appliances that most people could not afford before.

Brighter colors were chosen for walls and ceilings, replacing the browns and greens commonplace in the prewar period. Everything was "contemporary"—a word over-used by advertisers. Contrasting designs of wallpaper, curtains, carpets, and furnishings were encouraged.

Style on the road

The ambition of almost every family was to own a television and a car. Cars in particular were advertised constantly as the "dream purchase," with the family car pictured being washed, polished, shown off before admiring neighbors. Few people in the United States owned, or even saw, a foreign-built car. Out of all the cars sold in the United States, only 10 percent were foreign. In the early fifties many drivers were happy to buy used prewar models.

Above This 1952 advertisement describes the "dream kitchen," with garbage disposal and dishwasher. The manufacturer offers "beauty and unheard-of work savings" increasing the desire for better modern homes.

Above This 1950 Cadillac was basically the same as prewar designs. It was roomy, used lots of fuel, and was decorated heavily with chrome. Americans were still enjoying cheap gas, and "gas guzzlers" were not a problem.

Above *With the 1959 Mini, British designer Alec Issigonis produced a car that made its rivals look like oversized dinosaurs. The Mini was announced as a "baby car" but its low price and zippiness had an immediate appeal to young drivers. Its popularity endures.*

However, new models appeared every year; crowds flocked to auto shows and dealers' showrooms. While American cars got bigger and shinier, European cars got more compact. A European style breakthrough was Alec Issigonis's Mini (1959), a tiny front-engined car which was destined to be one of the symbols of the sixties. Less successful was the Ford Edsel (1957), the greatest financial flop in U.S. auto industry history.

Modernism

The fifties brought a new awareness of design. Wartime austerity and utility were replaced by styles that combined new materials with a look deliberately adopted for its "modernism." Abstract art moved into the commercial world, and design schools began to work much more closely with industry. Good design sells products; that was the message being spread throughout industry.

Certain phrases from the fifties are still with us: "gift department," "leisure clothing," "best-seller"—and, above all, "image"—public image, brand image, corporate image. Designers were more and more aware of the importance of creating an image that would win "customer loyalty." Modernism demanded new, snappy names; it was by design that the International Business Machines Corporation became simply the initials IBM. It was a sign of the times.

IMAGES OF THE FIFTIES

The shadow of the bomb

America was the world's only nuclear power until 1950, when the Soviet Union claimed to have its own atomic bomb. In October 1952 Britain tested an A-bomb and a month later the United States exploded the world's first hydrogen bomb at Eniwetok Atoll in the Pacific. The new weapon was far more powerful than the atomic bombs dropped on Japan in 1945, and its mushroom cloud sent a wave of apprehension around the world.

The Russians were quick to counter with an H-bomb of their own. The two superpowers now had weapons terrible enough to destroy not only each other, but the entire planet. "Mutual assured destruction" became the philosophy behind the nuclear deterrent.

Above *The mushroom cloud of the first H-bomb test in 1952 ushered in a new era of armed insecurity.*

Boeing wins the jet race

Boeing's four-engined 707 airliner first flew in July 1954. It was not the first jet plane to enter service. Britain's DeHavilland Comet had made its maiden flight in 1949 and began carrying passengers in May 1952. But a series of accidents in 1954 caused the Comet to be temporarily withdrawn from service, and it was Boeing which picked up the commercial prizes. More than 900 707s were built, and many are still flying.

The 707's capacity (167 passengers), range (it could fly nonstop from New York to London), and speed (cruising at 608 mph) brought in a new age of air travel. It halved the flight time across the Atlantic, and its success signaled the end for both piston-engined airliners and trans-Atlantic ocean liners such as the *Queen Elizabeth* and *United States*.

Below *Boeing's four-jet 707 airliner profited from the misfortunes of its rival, De Havilland's Comet. With jet travel, inexpensive vacations in distant lands became a reality.*

Raising the independence flag

On March 6, 1957, the Gold Coast, in West Africa, became the first British colony in Africa to achieve independence. The British flag was lowered and the flag of the new nation, renamed Ghana, was raised in its place. Ghana's first president was Kwame Nkrumah, who was to be prominent among a new generation of Third World leaders. Britain's prime minister, Harold Macmillan, spoke of a "wind of change" in Africa. Britain's once-vast Empire was quickly shrinking. In fact, the world map was being redrawn, as the territories of the old Empire gained their independence during the late fifties and, especially, the early sixties. The French, Belgian, and Dutch colonies in Africa and Asia also started demanding independence and many new nations were formed as a result.

Right *Ghana's new leader, Dr. Kwame Nkrumah, salutes cheering crowds at midnight on March 6, 1957—independence day for another part of Britain's empire.*

Dawn of the space age

On October 4, 1957, the world heard a faint, but momentous sound; the "bleep bleep" signal of the world's first artificial satellite. Sputnik I, a spherical device 23 inches in diameter and weighing just about 184 pounds, was blasted into orbit around the Earth by a Soviet rocket.

The Russians' achievement startled Western scientists, some of whom had openly scoffed at the suggestion that spaceflight was yet possible. As Sputnik I circled the Earth, its radio signals heralding the new space age, American space scientists scrambled to launch their own satellite. The so-called "space race" between the world's two superpowers was about to begin.

Below *Cuba's new Marxist leader, Fidel Castro, 1959. Castro's battle dress, beard, and pistol symbolized revolution. One press agency commented warily, "Despite his glasses, he looks rather fierce."*

Above *The world's first space satellite, Sputnik 1, was a small globe bearing long radio antennae. It could do little but reveal its presence by a monotonous signal. Yet its launch marked a major advance in human progress.*

Revolution in America's backyard

The island of Cuba, long a haven for rich tourists, gamblers, and the underworld, was in the news throughout 1959. The corrupt dictatorship of Fulgencio Batista was overthrown by a Marxist revolution, led by a lawyer named Fidel Castro. The 32-year-old Castro became the ultimate Communist opponent for Americans, who viewed with alarm the prospect of a Communist state, armed and supplied by the Soviet Union, so close to the American mainland. The U.S. government feared Cuban-style revolutionaries would soon become active throughout Central and South America. Castro's lieutenant, Che Guevara, was to become a revolutionary hero of the sixties, while Castro himself has remained Cuba's leader for the last three decades.

Nuclear power

The fifties saw the beginning of nuclear power. In 1954 the U.S. launched its first nuclear-powered submarine, the *Nautilus*. The first large-scale nuclear generating plant was Britain's Calder Hall, opened in Cumbria on October 17, 1956. The first nuclear power plant in this country opened in 1957 and supplied power to Pittsburgh. The promise of infinite supplies of cheap

 Above *The British nuclear power establishment at Windscale (now Sellafield). Nuclear power was good news: a fire here in 1957 did not attract attention.*

electricity was a tempting one for a world recovering from the ravages of a world war. Few people foresaw the environmental hazards of nuclear waste. For most, the opening of Calder Hall seemed to herald a technological golden age.

Above *Edmund Hillary's photo shows Sherpa Tenzing on the summit of Everest. To many, this mountaineering triumph seemed to herald a new age of achievement.*

Everest conquered

As Britain prepared to celebrate the coronation of Queen Elizabeth on June 2, 1953, there came dramatic news of a long-awaited triumph. Mount Everest, the world's highest mountain, had finally been climbed, after seven unsuccessful attempts. Two mountaineers—a New Zealander, Edmund Hillary, and a Nepalese Sherpa, Tenzing Norgay—had done what so many brave climbers had tried and failed to accomplish. They were members of a Commonwealth expedition led by Colonel John Hunt. Hillary and Tenzing climbed up the final snow ridge to the summit at 9 A.M. on May 29. When they returned to their base camp, the news was flashed by radio around the world, most of the people in Great Britain hearing it on Coronation Day itself.

The Suez crisis

The Suez Canal is a vital international waterway. In 1956 Egypt's President Nasser threatened to nationalize it (the Canal had been run since 1875 by a British-controlled company). Britain and France, fearing they would be cut off from trade with India and the Far East and acting secretly with Israel, staged a brief and unsuccessful invasion of the Canal zone. When the United States refused to back their action, they were forced to withdraw. Egypt took over the running of the Canal and the mishandled affair led to the resignation of Britain's prime minister, Anthony Eden.

Above *A British reconnaissance photo shows bombed fuel tanks burning near the Suez Canal during the military conflict of 1956, which ended ignominiously.*

Marching for equality

For many years minority groups in this country (blacks, Indians, Hispanics, and others) had suffered from discrimination. Education was a key issue in the fifties. In 1954 the U.S. Supreme Court declared that segregation of blacks and whites into separate schools must end. Discrimination in housing and jobs was also condemned. But court rulings did not bring about instant equality. Blacks took to the streets to demand civil rights for all.

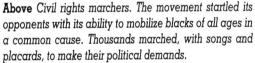

Above *Civil rights marchers. The movement startled its opponents with its ability to mobilize blacks of all ages in a common cause. Thousands marched, with songs and placards, to make their political demands.*

From 1956 the civil rights movement had a new and inspiring leader in the Reverend Martin Luther King, Jr. He led the struggle in the southern states, where segregation was more evident, as the movement gathered momentum for the massive campaigns and victories of the sixties.

Above *Defiance in Budapest, as Hungarians burn a Soviet flag to show their resistance shortly before Soviet forces invaded and quelled the uprising.*

The Hungarian uprising

Since the end of World War II Hungary, like other Eastern European states, had been in the iron grip of Soviet rule. Its Communist government was very unpopular and in October 1956 huge crowds flocked into the streets of Budapest, the Hungarian capital, demanding reforms and the removal of all Soviet troops from the country.

At first it seemed the Hungarians might win their freedom, but in November Budapest was stormed by Russian tanks. The revolt was brutally crushed, and thousands of Hungarians fled the country as refugees. A Soviet "puppet," Janos Kadar, was installed to head the Hungarian government; ex-premier and moderate Imre Nagy was seized and later executed for "treason."

An end to the polio scare

In the early fifties many young people lived in fear of an epidemic of polio. Polio (poliomyelitis) is a viral infection that affects the brain and nervous system. Outbreaks were worst in warm weather, and victims were often left paralyzed. Some spent months or years in iron lungs so they could breathe. Children were warned to avoid swimming pools and overexertion in sports during epidemics (which occurred in several years following World War II).

In 1955 the first American children were given an antipolio vaccine that had been developed by Dr. Jonas Salk. A British vaccine similar to Salk's was first used in 1956 and from 1958 an oral vaccine has been available. Immunization was a great success, ending the fear of the hot-summer polio epidemic—though it is still important today for children to be vaccinated against the disease.

Above *Dr. Jonas Salk, whose polio vaccine saved many lives. His own sons were among the first to be given experimental injections.*

War in Korea

The Korean War of 1950 to 1953 was the major fifties clash between East and West. In 1945 Korea (occupied by Japan during World War II) had been divided. The North had a Communist government under Soviet influence. The South was non-Communist and backed by the United States.

In 1950 Communist troops from North Korea invaded the South, and the "cold war" between the superpowers was fanned into flame. United Nations forces, mostly Americans but joined by troops from 15 other UN members including Britain, Canada, and Australia, were

 Above *A U.S. mortar in action during the Korean War. About 480,000 Americans fought in Korea, of whom some 157,000 were either killed or wounded.*

sent to repel the invasion. Communist China sent a "volunteer army" to aid the North Koreans and U.S. Sabres clashed with Russian-built Chinese MiGs in the very first jet dogfights. The war ground on both sides achieving sizeable gains of territory, but neither side was able to force a victory. The Panmunjon treaty in 1953 finally brought a truce, but no peace settlement was arrived at. The two Koreas have remained mutually hostile ever since, and negotiators are still trying to end the conflict.

GLOSSARY

Affluence An abundant supply of money, property, or wealth.

Anarchy Disorder or chaos resulting from the absence or failure of government. Anarchists believe in a totally free society, without government.

Austerity When consumer goods and luxuries are in short supply.

Civil rights movement The campaign by blacks to win full equality under the Constitution.

Cold War The period of antagonism between the Communist East, led by the USSR, and the West, the United States and its allies. It reached its height during the early 1950s.

Communism A political theory aiming to establish a society where the major enterprises such as factories, mines, farms, and stores are owned by all citizens rather than a class of wealthy people. In practice, Communist societies have tended to create powerful state authorities that control those enterprises.

Conscription (or draft) Compulsory enlistment in the armed forces.

Contraceptive A device used to prevent pregnancy.

Coronation The crowning of a monarch. Queen Elizabeth II was crowned on June 2, 1953.

Epidemic A word to describe a disease contracted by many people at the same time.

European Economic Community (EEC) An association of Western European countries, brought into being by the Treaty of Rome (1957) signed by France, West Germany, Italy, Belgium, Luxembourg, and the Netherlands. The United Kingdom, the Irish Republic, and Denmark joined in 1973, and Spain, Portugal, and Greece are also now members.

Four-minute mile A long-sought-after record in running. Roger Bannister became the first person to run a mile in under four minutes in May 1954.

Haute couture French for "high fashion."

Homosexual Someone sexually attracted to members of the same sex; particularly a man who is attracted to other men. Women attracted to other women are often called lesbians.

Immunization Protecting people from a disease, usually through an injection.

Nationalize To put an industry under the control of the state.

Segregation The separation of people according to race, as practiced in some states during the fifties, and in South Africa to this day.

Pacifism The belief that all forms of violence are wrong, and that people should not fight in wars.

Payola Bribes paid to persuade a DJ to play certain records on the radio.

Permissiveness A view of life which holds that people should be allowed to do as they please, with as little interference as possible.

Pop art A form of art glorifying the modern, mass-produced images of comics, TV, and advertising.

Rationing Restricting the distribution of goods that are in short supply. In Britain many things were rationed during World War II, and rationing did not end until 1954.

Sexual stereotyping The assumption that men and women have certain fixed roles in society; for example, that men go out to work while women stay at home as housewives and mothers.

Synthetic Something which is made artificially.

Tin Pan Alley A district in a city associated with the production of popular music. Originally it referred to an area of New York. It is mainly used to described "commercial" popular music prior to rock'n'roll.

FURTHER READING

The Crucial Decade and After: America 1945-1960, Eric F. Goldman (Random House, 1961)

The Glory and the Dream: A Narrative History of America 1932-1972, William Manchester (Little Brown, 1974)

God's Country: America in the Fifties, Ronald J. Oakley (Dembner Books, 1986)

Dick Clark's First Twenty Five Years of Rock and Roll, Michael Olsen and Bruce Solomon (Dell Books, 1981)

General background

America in the Twentieth Century, Frank Freidel (Alfred A. Knopf, 1965)

America in Our Time: From World War II to Nixon: What Happened and Why, Godfrey Hodgson (Doubleday, 1976)

Picture Acknowledgments

Barnaby's Picture Library 8t, 31, 38; Camera Press 44t, 44b; Kobal Collection cover left, lower right, 14t, 20t, 20b, 21, 22t; Novosti 40b; Peter Newark 6b, 7, 11, 26, 27, 35t; Photri 35b, 37, 43; Popperfoto cover, upper right, 5, 9t, 10, 16, 24, 25t, 25b, 29t, 33t, 45; TOPHAM 4, 6t, 8b, 9b, 12, 13, 14b, 15, 17, 18, 22b, 23, 28, 29b, 30, 32, 33b, 34, 36, 39, 40t, 41, 42t, 42b.

INDEX